Charlotte Brontë and Jane Eyre

by **Stewart Ross**

illustrated by **Robert Van Nutt**

For Charlotte (the other one)
with much love
S. R.

For the two literary geniuses born on April 21,
Charlotte Brontë and my wife, Julia
R. V. N.

VIKING
Published by the Penguin Group
Penguin Putnam Inc., 375 Hudson Street, New York, New York 10014, U.S.A.
Penguin Books Ltd, 27 Wrights Lane, London W8 5TZ, England
Penguin Books Australia Ltd, Ringwood, Victoria, Australia
Penguin Books Canada Ltd, 10 Alcorn Avenue, Toronto, Ontario, Canada M4V 3B2
Penguin Books (N.Z.) Ltd, 182-190 Wairau Road, Auckland 10, New Zealand

Penguin Books Ltd, Registered Offices: Harmondsworth, Middlesex, England

First published in 1997 by Viking, a member of Penguin Putnam Inc.

1 3 5 7 9 10 8 6 4 2

Text copyright © Stewart Ross, 1997
Illustrations copyright © Robert Van Nutt, 1997
All rights reserved

LIBRARY OF CONGRESS CATALOGING-IN-PUBLICATION DATA
Ross, Stewart. Charlotte Brontë and Jane Eyre / Stewart Ross; illustrated by Robert Van Nutt.   p. cm.
Includes bibliographical references and index. Summary: A biography of Charlotte Brontë, an English author, with emphasis on the
autobiographical material found in Jane Eyre.
ISBN 0-670-87486-8
1. Brontë, Charlotte, 1816-1855—Juvenile literature. 2. Women novelists, English—19th century—Biography—Juvenile literature. 3. Brontë, Charlotte,
1816-1855. Jane Eyre—Juvenile literature.
4. Autobiographical fiction, English—History and criticism—Juvenile Literature. [1. Brontë, Charlotte, 1816-1855. 2. Authors, English. 3. Women—
Biography. 4. Brontë, Charlotte, 1816-1855. Jane Eyre.] I. Van Nutt, Robert, ill. II. Title. PR4168.R65 1997 823'.8—dc21 [B] 97-1765 CIP AC

Manufactured in China. Set in Stempel Garamond.
Book design by Eileen Rosenthal.

AUTHOR'S NOTE

This book is about communicating enthusiasm for one of the finest stories ever written. While working on it, I had in mind two young readers. Reader One had read *Jane Eyre* and fallen under the Brontë spell. This reader now wanted to know more about the novel and the woman who wrote it. Where, for example, had she gotten her ideas? How much of Charlotte Brontë was there in her heroine? And how had the stuffy Victorian public reacted to her quiet feminist message? By answering such questions, I hoped to deepen Reader One's understanding and enjoyment of the work —and perhaps even persuade them to pick it up again.

My Reader Two had not read *Jane Eyre*. Perhaps put off by the book's size and rather old-fashioned language, this reader had opted for an "easier" read. My aim was to persuade them of the error of their ways.

In some respects, therefore, this book is an appetizer. I have prepared the literary taste buds for the main course—*Jane Eyre*—by telling the remarkable story of Charlotte Brontë's life, using both modern works and sources from her own time. I have pulled no punches. Charlotte was a woman of genius, but she had her faults. I have also suggested how the events of her life influenced her masterpiece. This is more tricky. The novel is fiction, presented as the autobiography of Jane Eyre, not Charlotte Brontë. But as writers can draw only from their own experience, filtered by imagination, it is hardly surprising to find that Jane and Charlotte had much in common.

After learning about these two overlapping lives—one real, the other imaginary— I hope those who have not already done so will read *Jane Eyre* itself. If they do, I promise they will not be disappointed.

Stewart Ross

Haworth

Spring comes late to the north of England.

A damp wind had been buffeting the town of Haworth all morning. Toward midday a heavy cart rumbled through the lower town and began the long climb up Main Street toward the parsonage. A few yards up the hill, the horse slipped on the wet cobbles. The driver opened his mouth to curse, then thought better of it. Oaths were not what the new parson and his family would want to hear. Not on their first day in Haworth.

The Reverend Patrick Brontë jumped down from the seat beside his wife. At forty-three he was still fit and strong. He strode up the steep slope without difficulty, nodding to bystanders who gathered to catch a glimpse of the clergyman and his family.

Maria Brontë was six years younger than her husband. In her arms lay three-month-old Anne, wrapped in a thick shawl to protect her from the raw April weather. The rest of the children, all under seven, perched among the piled boxes and trunks.

The eldest child, baptized Maria after her mother, was resting her arm protectively around the two-year-old Emily. Excited by the adventure, the red-headed Branwell was chattering with his sister Elizabeth. Charlotte, a year older than Branwell, sat at the back of the cart. The four-year-old girl stared in wide-eyed silence at the dirty side streets and cramped cottages of the small industrial town where she was destined to spend much of the rest of her life.

✣ ✣ ✣

The Brontë family moved to Haworth in April 1820. The parsonage where they lived stood midway between natural beauty and human squalor. To the rear stretched clear, broad moorland. On the other side the township sprawled up the hill like an ugly sore. Most families shared an outhouse with their neighbors, and the main street was awash with sewage. Disease lurked in every filthy corner. The average age of death was twenty-five; almost half the children died before their sixth birthday. The young Charlotte was to see more funerals than parties.

Shortly after the family's arrival, Mrs. Brontë fell gravely ill. When incurable stomach cancer was diagnosed, her sister Elizabeth Branwell came from Cornwall to help run the household. On September 15, 1821, with all her family gathered at her bedside, Maria Brontë groaned, "Oh God, my poor children!" Minutes later, she was dead.

✣ ✣ ✣

The family was deeply upset by Maria's death. But early death was a fact of life in those days, and in time the children got over their loss. For the next three years their father, helped by his sister-in-law and two servants, raised and educated the six children on his own. Although a kindly woman, Aunt Branwell was rather too strict for Charlotte's liking. It was her gentle and talented elder sister Maria that she thought of as her new mother, not her bossy aunt.

The children lived a strange life. Their Irish father was an outsider in Yorkshire. He made things more difficult by calling himself a gentleman and refusing to mix socially with the lower-class families of the mill workers. But as he earned only 180 pounds a year (enough to live on, but not for luxuries), he was not one of the local gentry either. So Charlotte and her brother and sisters grew up cut off from the world around them. This greatly affected Charlotte. In later life she often complained of the injustice of judging people on their backgrounds alone.

Patrick Brontë's duties as a clergyman kept him very busy. Even so, he always made time for his children. He ate breakfast and dinner with them. He guided their prayers and their reading—the whole family were great readers—and taught them history and geography. Whenever he could, he joined them for the high point of their day—lively romps over the sweeping moors.

The natural landscape made a deep impression on the young Charlotte. Many years later she wrote how Jane Eyre, fleeing from the deceitful human world, found peace in the "golden desert" of the "spreading moor." Nature was steadfast and true. To the orphan Jane it was a "universal mother" that loved her when the world did not. There were times when Charlotte, Jane's creator, must have felt the same.

Since all the Brontë children had powerful imaginations, there was never a dull moment when they played together. Their favorite indoor pursuits were making up games and stories and performing plays they had written. The central character was always the Duke of Wellington, Charlotte's hero, who had defeated Napoleon at Waterloo. If her brother or sisters ever suggested replacing the Duke with Napoleon or Julius Caesar, there would be an argument. Then Patrick would have to come out of his study to sort things out.

But these busy, joyful days could not last. Toward the end of 1823, Patrick decided that Aunt Branwell and he could no longer manage the children's education alone. He knew that only two careers were open to middle-class girls with no money—teaching or being a governess. Both required formal education.

For their own sakes, it was time for the Brontë girls to go to school.

In 1824 Patrick noticed an advertisement for Cowan Bridge, a new boarding school for the daughters of clergymen. Set up by the Reverend Carus Wilson, it was cheap and respectable and promised a good education. Maria and Elizabeth went there in July. Charlotte joined them in August and the six-year-old Emily in November.

It was probably the most unfortunate decision Patrick ever made in his life. A year's schooling for four at Cowan Bridge Clergy Daughters' School cost him 80 pounds and the lives of two daughters. The experience left Charlotte bitter and angry for the rest of her life.

Cowan Bridge was no worse than many nineteenth-century schools. The

DEADLY DISEASE

Many fatal diseases throve in the squalid towns of Victorian Britain. Among the worst were tuberculosis (which killed Charlotte's four sisters and her brother), typhoid (which probably killed Charlotte), typhus (which devastated Cowan Bridge School), and cholera. Nowadays they can all be cured with antibiotics. In Charlotte's day such drugs did not exist.

Tuberculosis, also known as T.B. or consumption, accounted for about 25 percent of all deaths in nineteenth-century Europe. A potentially fatal infection of the lungs spread through coughing or sneezing, it flourished in the crowded, ill-ventilated rooms of Cowan Bridge School. Victims cough (sometimes bringing up blood), lose weight, and run a fever. Although children are now vaccinated against T.B., there are signs that it is increasing in deprived inner-city areas.

Typhoid, caught from infected food or water, causes life-threatening fever and diarrhea. It spreads where sanitary systems are unsatisfactory. When Charlotte was born, for example, Haworth had not one toilet and only twenty-four outhouses. Sewage running down the main street polluted most of the drinking water.

Typhus is an infectious disease spread by lice. It causes headache, pain in the limbs, and a high fever. Victims die from pneumonia or heart or kidney failure.

Cholera epidemics devastated the insanitary towns of 19th-century Europe and America. It is caught from contaminated drinking water and results in violent vomiting and diarrhea. Victims may die within a few hours from dehydration.

cook was dreadful and one teacher, Miss Andrews, was very harsh. Once, when Maria Brontë was seriously ill, she got up only because she was afraid what Miss Andrews would say if she stayed in bed. In great pain, she dragged herself from under the covers and began to dress. The teacher, offended by the careless way the poor girl was putting on her clothes, hauled her into the middle of the room and shouted at her for being untidy. The hours were long and pupils had only one annual five-week vacation. On the other hand, they were quite well clothed and the standard of education was reasonable. Patrick, a sensitive man who cared deeply for his daughters, visited the school several times. He found little to complain about.

But Charlotte did.

To a lively eight-year-old who had never before been away from home, the school was prison. She had to wear a "charity girl" uniform and was allowed to write home only once every three months. The cook ruined the food. The dormitory was cold, the rules strict, the education narrow. Worse lay ahead.

Maria developed tuberculosis and during the long winter of 1824–25 bore her suffering with great bravery. By February she was too sick to remain at school. The frail eleven-year-old girl, Charlotte's "little mother," died in Haworth parsonage on May sixth.

By the end of the month, Cowan Bridge School was in the grip of a typhus epidemic and the pupils were moved to Carus Wilson's own house by the seaside. But as Charlotte and Emily rattled toward the coast, Elizabeth remained behind. A servant returned with her to Haworth where, on June 15, she, too, died of tuberculosis. Elizabeth was ten years old.

Charlotte was devastated. Two elder sisters whom she admired and loved deeply had been taken away to die apart from her. She stored her feelings in her heart, waiting to take a memorable revenge on Cowan Bridge, Reverend Carus Wilson, and the heartless Miss Andrews. In *Jane Eyre* she finally gave vent to her anger. The chapters on the terrible Lowood School, where the pupils are bullied unmercifully by the "cross and cruel" Miss Scatcherd and that "black column" of hypocrisy Mr. Brocklehurst, are as moving as anything she wrote.

✣ ✣ ✣

During the summer of 1825 the dwindling Brontë family was united once more in the parsonage. When not being taught by their father or aunt, the four remaining children read, played, and went for long walks. As before, they were quite happy to make their own entertainment.

In 1826 Branwell was given a box of toy soldiers. Immediately, the children gave them names (Charlotte called hers the Duke of Wellington, of course!) and started weaving stories around them, which they then wrote down. They called these tales the "History of the Young Men." They were full of thrilling adventures involving monsters, dungeons, dangerous escapes, and deeds of great bravery. In one year the young Brontës produced no less than eighteen tiny books, written in letters too small for adults to read. Inside was the children's own world—private, exciting, and fun.

By the age of twelve, Charlotte was already obsessed with writing. She said she would never marry, but devote her life to writing. In one of her stories from this time her beloved Duke of Wellington lost the power to speak and move. "Now," he said, "I dreaded that they would suppose I was dead & tried in vain to give some sign of life, the emotions of horror which filled my mind are unutterably describable." In the story the Duke is buried alive but

THE WORLD OF CHARLOTTE BRONTË

VICTORIAN BRITAIN—CHANGE AND INSECURITY

Charlotte Brontë lived during the reign of Queen Victoria (1837–1901), who became a symbol of stability at a time of rapid change. The population of Britain rose from about 13.5 million in 1831 to 32.5 million seventy years later. Industrial towns and cities grew rapidly. The rich became richer, exaggerating the gap between them and the poor. As construction ate up large areas of countryside, the idea of Nature became more highly regarded. Organized religion declined, and the loss sharpened the faith of believers. Rapid change in all walks of life bred a feeling of insecurity. Men and women responded by holding more tightly to what they knew.

The middle classes (about 7 percent of the population in 1830) felt particularly insecure. Caught between the powerful upper class and the huge, poor, and often ill-educated working class, they clung to traditional values: respectability, hard work, faith, and duty. These were the values of Patrick Brontë and his household.

CONFLICT AND REFORM

Change led to conflict. Reformers urged improvements of the worst aspects of the Industrial Revolution, such as child labor, pollution, and public health. Radical politicians demanded a society where ability was more important than class privilege. Charlotte herself wrote a partly "political" novel, *Shirley*.

However, she was more interested in social reform. Victorian women, particularly those from the middle class, were discriminated against in education, politics, employment, and marriage. They could not vote or stand for parliament, and they were legally bound to obey their husbands. Like her heroine Jane Eyre, Charlotte was most bitter about the narrow career opportunities open to women of her class. They were restricted to being either teachers or governesses. Although *Jane Eyre* is not a cry for revolution, behind the romantic plot lies a clear message: women and men are equal and should be treated as such.

rescued in the nick of time. Was Charlotte secretly wishing she could bring her dead sisters back to life, too?

The children learned their lessons fast, but it was a strange, lopsided education. They read widely and freely. Charlotte thoroughly enjoyed the poems of Lord Byron (usually considered too spicy for children) and sophisticated articles on literature and politics in the adult *Blackwood's Magazine.* Her father paid for private music and art lessons, and she picked up a little Latin and Greek. But she had virtually no formal scientific education. Her mathematics was basic, her knowledge of history and geography haphazard.

As a result, at fourteen Charlotte was only half educated. In some areas, such as literature, she had immense knowledge. In others, such as grammar and physics, she was an ignoramus. Above all, she lacked academic discipline. Like a volcano, her imagination poured out words, ideas, and images. Her spelling and punctuation were terrible. As the eldest child, who at any time might have to support her younger brother and sisters, she needed to go back to school.

✣   ✣   ✣

Patrick Brontë looked carefully at all the schools in the neighborhood and in 1831 eventually chose Roe Head. After the misery and pain of Cowan Bridge, the school was a delight. It was set in an attractive house some twenty miles southeast of Haworth, and the headmistress, Margaret Wooler, was intelligent and caring. Charlotte kept in touch with her for the rest of her life.

Charlotte took a few weeks to settle in. She was haunted by memories of Cowan Bridge and was teased for her simple dress, short sight, and plain appearance. She was not a handsome girl. Her face was heavy and round, her teeth crooked, and her hair a common brown. Like the heroine of *Jane Eyre,* she felt "humbled" by her "physical inferiority" to the other pupils.

But what Charlotte lacked in looks, she made up for in personality. Once she had found her feet, she showed herself to be lively, extremely smart, and a good organizer. She knew how difficult it was for her father to pay the school fees, and so she worked very hard. It was her duty, she announced, to get as much out of the school as she possibly could.

Roe Head gave Charlotte more than knowledge and academic training. It taught her conventional manners. Her strong Irish accent was a sign of social inferiority in snobbish Victorian England, so she learned to tone it down. More importantly, Roe Head brought her lasting friendships with two fellow pupils. Ellen Nussey, from a family of respected local business people, was warm, considerate, and dutiful. She was not as intelligent as Charlotte, but they shared many of the same opinions. Mary Taylor was quite different. She was independent, sharp, original, and painfully honest. The two girls represented the opposite sides of Charlotte's personality: duty and independence, intellect and instinct.

Charlotte spent a year and a half at Roe Head. During that time she became the school's star pupil, winning the silver medal for achievement for three consecutive terms. When she returned home to continue her own education and tutor Branwell, Emily, and Anne, she was still only sixteen.

Governess and Apprentice

CHARLOTTE REMAINED AT HAWORTH UNTIL SHE WAS NINETEEN. She gave lessons to Anne and Emily and continued her own education as best she could through reading. And she went on writing.

Branwell and Charlotte shared a passion for putting pen to paper—"scriblomania" they called it. They replaced the make-believe worlds of their childhood with the more adult Angria, where romance was just as important as adventure. But Angria was still unreal—a fantasy of mystery and love that lifted them out of the small world of Haworth. "I like high life," Charlotte wrote. "I like its manners, its splendors, its luxuries, the beings which move in its enchanted sphere."

In the company of the handsome men and beautiful women of Angria, Charlotte could forget her own plainness. Early on in *Jane Eyre* the servant Abbot cruelly describes Jane as "a little toad." Was this how the author saw herself when she glanced in the mirror each morning?

Writing was not Charlotte's only recreation. She still enjoyed walking on the moors, often accompanied by the family dog, Grasper. From time to time she went out to tea or acted as hostess to her father's guests. In the evenings she read, played games with her brother and sisters, or attended local concerts. In 1834 Patrick bought a piano. Charlotte liked playing, but her short sight made it difficult for her to read the music without leaning right over the keyboard.

Charlotte remained awkward in company she did not know. She was embarrassed by her appearance and lack of grace. A most difficult experience was going to stay with the Nusseys in their grand country house. Once, taking a gentleman's arm to be led into dinner, she was so nervous that she almost burst into tears. Later, when Ellen came to stay at Haworth, she found the parsonage bleak and dreary compared to her own comfortable home. She was amazed that Charlotte's father slept with a loaded pistol at his side and fired it out of the window every morning!

Patrick Brontë might have been eccentric, but he was also a surprisingly tolerant father. He was not a wealthy man, and the cost of keeping four children at home was considerable. Charlotte was now nineteen, and many fathers would have told her to get married or find regular employment rather than lose herself in the wonders of Angria. As a young man Patrick had tried a literary career himself, so he knew how difficult it was to make money by writing. For a woman it was almost impossible. He did not encourage Charlotte's literary ambitions, however, fearing they would end in frustration and unhappiness.

Charlotte was torn between duty and instinct. On one hand, she could say, "I am just going to write because I cannot help it." On the other hand, she felt compelled to follow what she called her "stern mistresses," Duty and Necessity. In July 1835 the "mistresses" got the upper hand, and she went off to teach at Roe Head school. She was accompanied by Emily, whose fees she paid out of her earnings.

✢ ✢ ✢

The Brontë children had little use for institutions or petty rules. It was as if the wild, unfettered spirit of the moors had somehow entered their souls, setting them apart from other people. Emily loathed Roe Head. Ill and unhappy, she returned home in October, and her place was taken by her fifteen-year-old sister, Anne. Charlotte, not a natural teacher, stuck to her task but grew more and more depressed and self-pitying. In frustration, she called her pupils "fat-headed oafs"! She left the school in 1837, but returned the following year. By Christmas, she had finally had enough and came home to Angria and the familiar, eccentric parsonage.

It was not just teaching that upset Charlotte. In 1836 she had sent some of her poems to the poet Robert Southey, asking his opinion of them. His reply was discouraging. While admitting that she had talent, he declared, "Literature cannot be the business of a woman's life, and it ought not to be." Charlotte did not agree with him, but she had seen the sort of prejudice she had to fight against.

A weaker character than Charlotte might have taken Southey's advice and given up. She could easily have dropped the idea of writing and followed the conventional life of a wife and mother. She had the chance to do this shortly after she stopped teaching. In March 1839 Ellen Nussey's twenty-six-year-old brother, Reverend Henry Nussey, wrote to Charlotte proposing marriage. The clergyman's proposal was more like a business offer than the declaration of passion Charlotte had dreamed of, and she turned him down. She also rejected David Bryce, a lively young clergyman whom she considered socially inferior to her. (Although she hated Victorian prejudice, when it came to choosing a husband she could be quite a snob herself.) Nevertheless, turning down two proposals of marriage was not easy. She was not attractive and knew they might well be the only offers she would ever receive.

At about this time Charlotte sent the beginning of one of her stories to Hartley Coleridge, the son of the famous poet. He did not think it worth publishing. The only pleasure Charlotte got from their correspondence was that he could not decide from her writing whether she was a man or a woman.

Having rejected teaching and marriage, the only thing Charlotte had left to try was being a governess. It was hardly an exciting option. When Jane Eyre decides to leave Lowood School and become a governess, she calls it moving to "a new servitude." This was precisely how Charlotte found her change of situation.

She made two attempts at being a governess, first with a local family, then with a merchant in Bradford. Neither was a success. She found the children hard to control and her work humiliating and boring. She loathed being asked to do menial housework such as sewing. The problem was that she knew she was far more able than her wealthier employers and so could not accept her lowly status. "A private governess," she exploded in a letter to Emily, "has no existence." In making the heroine of *Jane Eyre* a governess, Charlotte launched a famous protest at the way such people were treated.

In the summer of 1841 Aunt Branwell came to the rescue. She offered to put up money for Charlotte, Emily, and Anne to set up their own school. At first Charlotte was very keen on the scheme. Then an even better idea came to her. She had recently heard from her old friend Mary Taylor, who was in Brussels on a European tour. Brussels! The very word filled Charlotte with hope. It stood for excitement, freedom, and challenge. She told her aunt that before they started a school, the girls needed to finish their education abroad. Brussels, where the Taylors were, was just the place, and Charlotte and Emily could go together.

When Charlotte was in such a mood, nothing could stand in her way. When Jane Eyre said "I am going!" she meant it. So, too, her creator. Aunt Branwell, Patrick, and Emily were won around. A suitable school, the Pensionnat Heger, was found and on February 8, 1842, Charlotte and Emily, in the company of their father, took the train south for London and the ferry to Belgium.

❖ ❖ ❖

Charlotte's stay in Brussels changed her life. Far from domestic responsibilities, she had a host of exciting new experiences—overseas travel, different food and culture and, above all, a teacher she really respected. Monsieur Constantin Heger was lively and highly intelligent. He did not teach Charlotte to write, but he taught her to think closely about the craft of writing. Under his guidance she became a true novelist, a writer of power, style, and originality. But it cost a great deal of hard work. And heartache.

Madame Claire Heger ran the Pensionnat Heger for girls, with her husband Constantin as the principal teacher. At first Charlotte and Emily found it tough going. They were much older than the other pupils. The language of instruction was French, and the Brontës were the only Protestants. Despite these difficulties, Monsieur Heger was delighted with their progress. At the end of six months—the period that Aunt Branwell had paid for—Charlotte suggested they remain at the Pensionnat and pay their fees by doing some teaching. Pleased to keep such promising pupils, the Hegers agreed.

Emily was no teacher and Charlotte was not much better, but both—particularly Charlotte—found Monsieur Heger's instruction highly stimulating. His method was to analyze pieces of famous French literature in depth. They examined every aspect of it—the ideas, the choice of words, the way the sentences and paragraphs were put together, and even the punctuation. The students then wrote their own pieces in the style of the original. Monsieur Heger commented on their work with sharp understanding.

On November 2, 1842, Charlotte learned that Aunt Branwell was seriously ill. She died the following day and the sisters returned home for Christmas. Afterward Emily chose to remain with her elderly father. Charlotte went back to Brussels alone and was soon hard at work again. It was not just schooling that had drawn her back. Day by day, week by week, she was falling in love with the ugly, passionate, vigorous Constantin Heger.

The truth of what passed between Charlotte and her married teacher will never be known. While she was obsessed by him, he thought highly of her talents but probably no more. Charlotte's love was doomed. By the autumn of 1843 she had become bitter and lonely. She criticized her pupils and grew to hate Madame Heger. Only her beloved teacher was above criticism. Finally, brokenhearted, she could take no more and on December 31 she left for England. She had never felt more wretched in her life.

Currer Bell

BACK IN HAWORTH, CHARLOTTE MOONED ABOUT THE PARSONAGE, writing frequent, intense letters to her "professor," Monsieur Heger. His friendly but cool replies gave her no hope that her love would be returned. What was she to do? She had neither job, husband, nor fortune. The 300 pounds left her by Aunt Branwell would not keep her for the rest of her life, and she was already thirty. "My Youth," she mourned to her friend Ellen Nussey, "is gone like a dream." Charlotte was also worried about her father, who was going blind.

Seeking excitement to lift her out of her wretchedness, Charlotte even thought of going to Paris as a governess. As it was, her only adventure during the summer of 1845 was visiting Ellen Nussey at Hathersage in Derbyshire, where Ellen's brother Henry was vicar.

The three-week visit stuck in Charlotte's memory. She remembered the dramatic, bleak scenery, the memorials to the Eyre family in Hathersage church and the Eyre family home of North Lees Hall. She remembered, too, talking with Ellen about her brother George, who was in a mental asylum, and Henry Nussey's cold proposal of marriage to her. All this she stored in her mind and used in *Jane Eyre*.

✤ ✤ ✤

That July Branwell was dismissed from his post as a tutor. Anne, who had been a governess in the same household, had left of her own accord a month earlier. What had gone wrong?

Branwell, of whom so much had been expected, was proving to be a bitter

LITERARY BACKGROUND TO *Jane Eyre*

In the early 1700s Daniel Defoe and Samuel Richardson wrote the first English novels. By Charlotte's time the fashion was for long novels in three volumes. Some first appeared in magazines, one chapter at a time.

Charlotte's favorite reading was the King James Bible and the works of William Shakespeare, John Bunyan, and John Milton. *Jane Eyre* has many references to all four. She also devoured the poetry of the Romantic poets, especially William Wordsworth, Samuel Taylor Coleridge, and Lord Byron. They—and her own personality—are the sources of the romantic passion in *Jane Eyre*.

Charlotte was less influenced by novelists. She admired the popular works of Walter Scott and of Charles Dickens, the leading novelist of her day. The Lowood School chapters in *Jane Eyre* are Dickensian in effect and sentiment, recalling the ghastly Dotheboys Hall in Dickens' *Nicholas Nickleby*. Other parts of *Jane Eyre*—such as Jane hearing Rochester's voice calling her from many miles away—show the influence of Gothic novels, mystical stories of magic and the supernatural, of which the best-known example is Mary Shelley's *Frankenstein*.

Novel writing was the one branch of literature in which women were taken seriously—as long as their works were morally correct and their heroes and heroines virtuous. Surprisingly, Charlotte did not come across the work of fellow women novelists until rather late in life. When she wrote *Jane Eyre* she had not even read the works of Jane Austen.

Jane Eyre was a most original novel. This was one reason for its success. It was no Gothic horror or tale of domestic manners. It was as unlike the historical yarns of Scott as it was the vigorous, sprawling works of Dickens. In short, as one critic put it, it was "an extraordinary book...unlike all that we have read."

Branwell, a talented artist, painting a portrait of the Brontë children.

disappointment. Although his lively and imaginative mind teemed with dreams and schemes, he lacked Charlotte's iron will. He had failed as a portrait painter, tutor, and railway clerk. Now he had been dismissed again, for carrying on a love affair with Mrs. Lydia Robinson, his employer's wife.

Depressed and out of work, he kept away from home. He still wrote a little, but wasted most of his time on drink and opium. His father was heartbroken, Charlotte unforgiving. Perhaps she was jealous of her brother, whose poems had been published in the newspapers? He had, after all, experienced some success in the two areas where she had failed: love and authorship.

There was not much Charlotte could do to match her brother as a lover, but she was determined not to be outshone by him as a writer. In the autumn of 1845 she sneaked a look at some of Emily's poems. They were, she decided, excellent, and she had the idea of cooperating with her sisters to publish a book of verse. Emily agreed, although she was angry with Charlotte for reading her work. Anne also came in on the project. When he learned what had happened, Branwell was bitterly upset at being left out.

Now that she had something positive to do, Charlotte's depression lifted. She found—and paid—a publisher, and in 1846 the *Poems* of Currer, Ellis, and Acton Bell appeared. The sisters used male pen names to avoid the Victorian prejudice against women poets. If they had given their real names, most readers would have judged them first as women and only second as writers.

The change of name did not help much. *Poems* received some favorable reviews—and sold two copies.

Undaunted, the sisters concentrated on their prose. They worked together, sometimes writing in the same room and reading their work out loud to each other. Emily called her story *Wuthering Heights*. Anne's was *Agnes Grey*. Charlotte worked on *The Professor,* a story based on her time in Brussels. The three books were sent off together to various publishers. After a year *Wuthering Heights* and *Agnes Grey* had been accepted for publication, on condition that the authors put up 50 pounds each. This would be returned if the books sold well. For Charlotte's novel, however, no home was found.

Charlotte wanted desperately to earn a living by her pen, so she refused to pay to have *The Professor* published. Moreover, if her first novel was not quite

what the market wanted, she had another waiting to be written. The ideas and inspiration were all there. All she needed was an opportunity.

In August 1846 Charlotte took her father to Manchester for an operation to restore his sight. It was a success, but afterward Patrick had to remain with his eyes bandaged for several weeks. During this period, living in hired rooms in Manchester, Charlotte began her second novel. She called it *Jane Eyre*.

The story had been growing in Charlotte's mind since 1844. Now that she had begun it, writing in pencil in little square books, it almost wrote itself. The make-believe world of her childhood was gone forever. In its place was the realm of Charlotte's personal experience, based on landscapes she had seen and people she had met.

Charlotte had not given up hope of finding a publisher for *The Professor*. In July 1847 she sent it to Smith, Elder & Co. of London. They replied saying they liked the book but did not feel it was suitable for publication. Charlotte sighed and glanced through the rest of the letter. Her heart jumped. If Currer Bell had a three-volume novel, the publishers wrote, they would like to see it. Of course she had a three-volume novel!

Charlotte finished *Jane Eyre* in a rush and sent it off to Smith, Elder & Co. on August 24. The manuscript was handed to several readers for their opinion. Every one of them was delighted with it. Intrigued, George Smith, one of the owners of the firm, took it home one Saturday evening. After breakfast the following morning he carried the manuscript into his study to have a look at it. By the time he went to bed that night, he had read every word.

Charlotte Brontë's heroine, Jane Eyre, meeting her mysterious employer, Mr. Rochester.

Jane Eyre

THE HANDWRITTEN MANUSCRIPT THAT SO CAPTIVATED GEORGE SMITH was presented as the autobiography of Jane Eyre. Charlotte liked the name Eyre, which she had noticed in Hathersage church, because it suggested a heroine as free as *air* and *heir* to a fortune. The spirited Jane is a ten-year-old orphan in the care of her selfish widowed aunt, Mrs. Reed. The abused child's honesty and intelligence contrast starkly with the selfishness of the family that has been forced to adopt her, and she wins the reader's sympathy from the very first page.

Although small, thin, and plain (like Charlotte), Jane has the heart of a giant. She is cruelly punished for fighting back when bullied by her cousins Eliza, Georgiana, and, particularly, John. Unable to break the child's spirit, Mrs. Reed decides to get rid of her by sending her away to a boarding school.

The orphan's appalling experiences at Lowood School are an exaggerated version of what happened to Charlotte at Cowan Bridge. The accommodation is bare and the food inedible. The behavior of some teachers, notably Miss Scatcherd (based on the dreaded Miss Andrews) is unnecessarily harsh. The school's treasurer and manager, the Reverend Mr. Brocklehurst, is a vicious hypocrite.

Jane has a choice. She can either rebel or, like her friend Helen Burns (perhaps a picture of Charlotte's beloved sister Maria), accept the cruelty with Christian bravery. But whether she wishes to or not, Jane simply *cannot* accept injustice. She is too passionate. Fortunately, she is very good at her studies and finds a friend and helper in the kind Miss Temple. After an outbreak of typhus, during which Helen Burns dies of consumption, the school is reformed and rebuilt, and taken out of Mr. Brocklehurst's control. (It is tempting to think that this is just what Charlotte wished had happened at Cowan Bridge.)

Now much happier, Jane stays at Lowood for six years as a pupil and two as a teacher. However, when Miss Temple leaves, Jane decides that she too must move on. She takes a post as a governess. On the eve of her departure, she is visited by Bessie, the most kindly of Mrs. Reed's servants. She tells Jane that John Reed has become a rich hooligan and that seven years previously Jane's uncle from Madeira had come looking for her.

❖   ❖   ❖

After a long journey, Jane arrives at Thornfield Hall (based on North Lees Hall or on the Rydings, both houses known to Charlotte), where she is to be governess to a young French girl, Adèle Varens. From the friendly housekeeper, Mrs. Fairfax, Jane learns that the property is owned by Mr. Edward Rochester, who is often absent. Jane settles happily into her new life but is mystified by Grace Poole, a reclusive servant who lives in the attic, and by the "tragic" and "mirthless" laughter she sometimes hears at the top of the house.

In due course, Rochester returns home. Jane meets him before he reaches the house, helping him when his horse falls on the icy road. The pale but determined little governess is immediately attracted to her broad, dark, and moody master. To her surprise, she finds him taking an interest in her, too. He praises her intelligence and honesty, and they begin to become friends.

One day Rochester explains to Jane that Adèle is the illegitimate daughter of a French actress, Céline, with whom he had an affair. Out of kindness he has adopted the child, though she in no way resembles him. That night, after Jane has bravely extinguished a fire mysteriously started in his bedroom, he confesses that the "expression" and "smile" in her eyes has delighted his "very inmost heart."

Now, when Jane believes she and Rochester are near to confessing their love, he leaves. In a letter he announces that a party of wealthy guests are coming to stay at Thornfield. Jane does her best to smother her disappointment. The guests include the snobbish Dowager Lady Ingram and her daughters Mary and the beautiful and talented Blanche. The company have little time for the insignificant-looking governess. (Charlotte was writing from the heart—she knew only too well what it was like to be a "disconnected, poor, and plain" governess.) When Rochester flirts openly with Blanche, Jane is hurt but not jealous—she thinks Blanche "too inferior" for jealousy, because she is "not genuine."

While Rochester is away, supposedly on business, a mysterious stranger named Mason arrives from the West Indies. Rochester returns, disguised as a gypsy fortune-teller. He is shaken by news of Mr. Mason's arrival. That night Mason is stabbed, apparently by Grace Poole. Rochester keeps the attack secret from everyone except Jane, who nurses him until Rochester arrives with a surgeon.

Believing Rochester is about to marry Blanche, Jane learns that John Reed is dead, and the dying Mrs. Reed wishes to see her. Jane visits her relatives, finding Georgiana empty-headed and lazy and Eliza obsessed with religious routine. Just before she dies, Mrs. Reed confesses that three years ago Jane's Uncle John from Madeira had written wishing to make Jane his heir. Mrs. Reed told him Jane had died at Lowood.

✦ ✦ ✦

Jane returns to Thornfield expecting to hear news of Rochester's planned marriage to Blanche. Unable to control her emotion, she tells him how delighted she is to be back. He is strangely cheerful. Eventually, on Midsummer Eve, Jane and Rochester meet alone in the garden. When Jane admits how heartbroken she will be when he marries Blanche, he confesses that Blanche is nothing to him. Their love is finally in the open, and they agree to marry. A violent thunderstorm matches Rochester's wild mood.

Jane shows her independence by remaining a governess until her wedding day. She also writes to her Uncle John in the hope that one day she will have some money of her own. She would then not have to put up with "being dressed like a doll by Mr. Rochester."

The night before her wedding day, Jane has troubling dreams. Worse, a horrible figure enters her bedroom, tries on her veil, and tears it in two. Mr. Rochester tries to convince her it was Grace Poole. There are no guests at the

wedding service, but two strangers slip in at the back. At the crucial moment they declare that the service cannot proceed because Rochester is already married. One of the men is a solicitor named Briggs, acting on behalf of a Mr. Eyre from Madeira. The other is Mr. Mason, who had been stabbed at Thornfield. Briggs reveals that many years ago Mason's sister—Bertha Mason —had married Rochester in Spanish Town, Jamaica. She is now insane and living under the protection of Grace Poole in the attic of Thornfield. She was responsible for the fire and the murderous attacks.

✢　✢　✢

Jane's life is shattered. Rochester explains how he had been tricked into marrying Bertha, a vicious and worthless woman. He asks Jane to live with him as his lover. She does not reject the idea out of hand, for she loves him dearly. But the still small voice of her conscience will not allow it. As Rochester's mistress, she would be completely dependent on him. She cannot accept that. Her relationship with him has to be a partnership between equals, or nothing.

Jane flees south to Derbyshire. Wretched and sick with exhaustion, "Jane Elliott" (as she now calls herself) is given shelter near the village of Morton. Her savior is the stern Reverend St. John Rivers, who is staying with his two sisters, Diana and Mary. Like the Brontë sisters, the three young women have much in common and get on very well. The family is disappointed to learn that a rich uncle has died and left them nothing. When Diana and Mary leave to work as governesses, Jane starts up an elementary school.

St. John Rivers rejects the advances of the pretty and able Rosamond Oliver. He then discovers Jane's true identity and what had happened at Thornfield. He reveals that the uncle who had left him and his sisters out of his will was Jane's uncle, John Eyre of Madeira. Jane and the Rivers are cousins, and she has been left 20,000 pounds! Jane calls Diana and Mary home and divides her fortune among the four of them. (One hundred fifty years ago the interest from 5,000 pounds—about 7,500 dollars—provided an ample income for life.)

St. John Rivers is preparing to go abroad as a missionary. He urges Jane to accompany and assist him as his wife. (Perhaps Charlotte recalled the cold marriage proposal she had received from Henry Nussey?) Jane refuses, but Rivers persists, urging her to put Christian duty before personal feeling. His powerful argument saps her will to resist. Just when she feels she can hold out no longer, she is set free by a mysterious call for help coming from nowhere—Rochester's voice crying, "Jane! Jane! Jane!" The spell of the marble-hearted missionary is broken, and the next day she leaves for Thornfield.

Jane finds that Thornfield has been destroyed in a fire started by Bertha Rochester. The madwoman died in the blaze. Trying to save her, Rochester lost a hand as well as his sight. Jane goes to him immediately. Now there is no shadow between them, and their love can blossom, pure and passionate. They are married at once, to the delight of Mary and Diana Rivers.

Concluding her story ten years later, Jane says that Adèle has matured into a fine young woman, and Mary and Diana are happily married. Their brother is on the verge of fulfilling his ambition, too—death in the service of God. Rochester's sight is partially restored. Jane bears his children and lives with him in perfect happiness, "bone of his bone and flesh of his flesh."

✣ ✣ ✣

The story, George Smith realized, was remarkable. He decided to write to Currer Bell, offering to publish *Jane Eyre* immediately.

Mrs. Nicholls

GEORGE SMITH OFFERED CHARLOTTE 100 POUNDS for Jane Eyre and the same for each of her next two novels. She accepted, but refused to make the changes Smith suggested, such as making the book's beginning less gloomy.

The novel was published in October 1847 and was an immediate success. By February 1848 it had been reprinted, and was adapted for the London stage. Only a few readers were critical. The *Spectator* magazine, for example, did not approve of its "low tone of behavior," meaning Jane was too passionate to be a respectable young woman. Most other reviewers thought the novel fresh, powerful, and interesting. They longed to know whether "Currer Bell" was a man or a woman.

The mystery deepened in December 1847 when Ellis Bell's *Wuthering Heights* and Acton Bell's *Agnes Grey* appeared. Some said the three Bells were the same person. Meanwhile, Emily and Anne had begun their second novels, while Charlotte had embarked on her third, *Shirley*. Anne's work was published as *The Tenant of Wildfell Hall*, but Emily's second novel has disappeared. Charlotte probably destroyed it after her sister's death, believing it was too racy!

Patrick was quietly proud of his daughters' success, but this did not make up for his sorrow at what was happening to his son. Branwell was now a physical and mental wreck. He slept in his father's room so the old man could watch over and comfort him. Charlotte, once her brother's closest companion, had no sympathy left for him. She understood his depression because she had the same tendency to dramatize her own feelings. But she saw his failure to control his emotions as weakness. Watching his tragic decline made her all the more determined to keep her own passions under control.

By the summer of 1848 the rumors about Currer, Ellis, and Acton Bell were getting out of hand. To sort things out, Charlotte and Anne went to London to meet their publishers for the first time. They came unannounced, so when George Smith heard that two shy little country ladies had called to see him, he was somewhat surprised. When his visitors revealed themselves, his surprise turned to amazement, then delight. He was fascinated by Charlotte. She looked so ordinary, he wrote later in his *Memoir*: a "very small," bespectacled woman, with a head rather too large for her body and a "quaint old-fashioned look." Yet a genius with the pen. Even so, he believed "she would have given all her genius and her fame to have been beautiful."

There was little beauty in Haworth at this time. Branwell was dying slowly and painfully of tuberculosis. A sense of failure hung over him. "In all my past life," he moaned, "I have done nothing either great or good." The man who had once been the leader and driving spirit of the Brontë children passed away in his father's arms, aged thirty-one, on September 24, 1848.

Anne and Emily were also unwell. Soon after Branwell's death it was clear that Emily had the same disease as her brother and would not live long. Charlotte, close to collapse, was swept by misery, self-pity, and illness. Day by day she watched helpless as "the nearest thing to my heart" coughed toward pale and wasted death. Emily's agony ended at two o'clock in the afternoon of December 19. She was buried three days later.

The Brontë tragedy was not yet over. By the spring Anne, too, was thin, pale, and racked by a painful cough. Smitten with grief, Charlotte recognized the horribly familiar symptoms of tuberculosis. On May 23, 1849, she and Ellen Nussey took Anne for a visit to the seaside town of Scarborough. The fresh air raised the invalid's spirits, but did nothing for her health. She died on May 28 and was buried beneath the ancient walls of Scarborough Castle.

Charlotte returned to Haworth with only her father for company and her writing to give her life meaning. "Why life is so blank, brief and bitter," she wrote in despair, "I do not know."

Shirley was published in October 1849 and sold well. The success helped lift
Charlotte out of her misery. Over the next two years she traveled frequently,
making several visits to London to stay with the handsome George Smith
and his mother. She was still uneasy in city society. At formal parties she was
either too timid or too direct, and she remained painfully aware of her rather
plain looks. She once tried to make herself more glamorous for a dinner party
by wearing a false hairpiece. The sophisticated guests thought it made her look
ridiculous and laughed about it for a long time afterward.

Charlotte made new friends, including fellow writers Harriet Martineau and
Elizabeth Gaskell. Year by year her fame grew. By 1850 it was well known, even
in remote Haworth, that she was Currer Bell, the author of the hugely popular
Jane Eyre. To Patrick's annoyance, the first tourists began calling at the parson-

age in the hope of meeting his remarkable daughter.

Charlotte was now working on a fourth novel, *Villette,* in which the heroine rejects a rather ordinary hero, Dr. John Bretton. Bretton's character was based on her publisher, George Smith—and he was not amused! He was a close friend of Charlotte's and it had even been rumored that one day they might marry.

George did not propose to Charlotte. Others did, however. She turned down one suitor because she said he looked too much like Branwell. The following year she rejected her father's curate, Arthur Bell Nicholls. For a long time she had not thought much of this rather dull-looking Irishman, whose "narrowness of mind" she scorned. But over the years, when she saw how kind he was to her father, her attitude softened. Nicholls was turning out to be less boring, too. He enjoyed her novels, laughing out loud at her criticisms of the clergy. In declaring his love for her he showed a deep and genuine passion.

The match was not to be—not for the moment, anyway. Patrick Brontë was set against it, and Charlotte used this as an excuse to turn Nicholls down. Heartbroken, he planned to become a missionary while his beloved took herself off to London. But she was not at ease. Her father had a second stroke, leaving him permanently disabled. The prospect of having to devote herself to his care for years loomed before her. It looked as if the love and domestic happiness that had eventually blessed Jane Eyre would pass by her creator for ever.

✣   ✣   ✣

Charlotte had not told Nicholls she would never marry him. So, thinking things over, he gave up the missionary idea and began to write to her in secret. She did not object and eventually told her father what was going on. Patrick disapproved strongly. He did not want to lose his one remaining daughter, particularly to someone he considered socially inferior. At the back of his mind he was probably also worried about Charlotte's health. If she married and became pregnant, the strain might prove too much for her frail body.

But Patrick had never been able to stop Charlotte when her mind was

made up. The letter-writing continued. In time she and Arthur Nicholls began to meet. Finally, in the spring of 1854 she accepted him as her husband. She did not yet love him, but she knew him to be a strong and kind man with a good sense of humor. For the moment that was enough.

The couple was married on June 29, 1854. After the honeymoon, they set up home in the parsonage, and for a few months Charlotte was happier than she had ever been in her life. After years of longing and misery, at last she felt the deep joy of being loved and cared for. In return, her affection for her husband grew and deepened.

By early in the new year Charlotte was expecting a child. As Patrick had feared, the strain of pregnancy at the age of thirty-nine taxed her strength to its limits. By February she had grown alarmingly thin and was vomiting blood. Ominously, she made her will, leaving all she had to her dearest husband.

The wasting sickness dragged painfully on until, by mid-March, all hope was gone. Early in the morning on the last day of the month, Charlotte Nicholls and her unborn child died. The funeral took place four days later. A large congregation gathered to say farewell to the frail genius who had made Haworth famous. In silence they watched her mortal remains lowered into the family vault beside those of her mother, her brother, and all but one of her sisters.

For days her father and husband were almost sick with grief. "All our hopes have ended in disappointment, and our joy in mourning," groaned Patrick. In his sorrow he could not see that his beloved, brilliant Charlotte had left the world a treasure that would last for all time.

THE HISTORY OF *Jane Eyre*

*S*mith, Elder & Co. of London published *Jane Eyre* in three separate volumes in October 1847. It was subtitled "An Autobiography. Edited by Currer Bell." Since then the novel has been reprinted countless times, translated into all the world's major languages, and often filmed. Although now 150 years old, it remains one of the most popular stories ever written.

On the whole critics liked *Jane Eyre* when it first appeared, although its originality surprised them. "Such a strange book!" wrote the reviewer in *Sharpe's Magazine.* "Imagine a novel with a swarthy governess for heroine, and a middle-aged ruffian for hero." Critics who disapproved of the book's "questionable" morality and "coarseness of language" had two main objections. First, Rochester was too sinful to be a worthy hero; second, Jane's straightforwardness, honesty, and passion made her not quite decent. Even those who approved of the book thought it too "adult" for children. A century ago it was still not thought suitable reading for young ladies. Today it is on the syllabuses of many English literature courses throughout the world.

ELIZABETH GASKELL AND THE BRONTË LEGEND

Charlotte Brontë and Elizabeth Gaskell first met in 1850. The two writers immediately became friends, and in September 1853 Elizabeth came to stay with Charlotte at Haworth. From that brief, four-day visit grew the famous "Brontë Legend."

Elizabeth Gaskell had thought of writing the story of Charlotte's life even while her friend was still alive. She took up the project in earnest shortly after Charlotte's death and went to visit Patrick Brontë and Arthur Nicholls. Throughout the interview both men were in tears. With a little persuasion, however, she got them to agree to help her. She made friends with Ellen Nussey and accepted her selection of Charlotte's letters. They gave "a very beautiful idea of her character," Elizabeth wrote in a letter of thanks. The biographer made a second visit to Haworth, and also contacted most people who had known Charlotte well. Some provided her with important letters. Others—such as George Smith—did not. From this random selection of material, Elizabeth Gaskell put together a wonderful book.

Gaskell's *Life of Charlotte Brontë* is well written and extremely moving. But the author was a novelist. She was more concerned with writing a good story than with seeking out the truth. With the best possible motives, she turned Charlotte into a long-suffering heroine. "All her life was but labour and pain," she wrote, "and she never threw down the burden for the sake of present pleasure."

The *Life of Charlotte Brontë* makes no mention of Charlotte's snobbery, or bossiness. There is no hint of her passionate love for Monsieur Heger, a married man. Branwell is turned into an untalented good-for-nothing and Patrick into a surly old ogre. Haworth is described as an isolated and backward country parish with an ancient, cold, and drafty parsonage. Charlotte herself, struggling against all odds to produce great literature in these ghastly circumstances, emerges as almost a saint.

Gaskell's *Life of Charlotte Brontë* became the most talked-about book in London. It caused bitter argument, particularly about the Cowan Bridge Clergy Daughters' School. Yet it was powerful enough to charm those who had once criticized Charlotte for being unladylike. She was now "poor Charlotte," a perfect example of the long-suffering, mild-mannered Victorian lady.

Fortunately, careful recent scholarship has stripped away the Victorian facade to reveal the true Charlotte Brontë. The picture is less elegant than the earlier one, but it is vastly more interesting.

CHRONOLOGY OF THE LIFE OF CHARLOTTE BRONTË

1816   Born in Thornton, Yorkshire, England, the third of six children.

1820   Family moves to nearby Haworth, Yorkshire.

1821   Aunt Branwell arrives from Cornwall. Mother, Maria Brontë, dies.

1824   At Cowan Bridge Clergy Daughters' School with Maria, Elizabeth, and Emily.

1825   Maria and Elizabeth die of T.B. Charlotte and Emily return home.

1825–31 Under Branwell's leadership develops fantastic world of childhood imaginings.

1831–32 At Roe Head School. Makes friends with Ellen Nussey and Mary Taylor.

1832–35 Living at home, teaching her sisters and writing the mythical Angrian sagas with Branwell.

1835–38 Teaching at Roe Head School.

1839   Rejects proposal of Reverend Henry Nussey. Works as a governess for the Sidgewick family. Rejects proposal of Reverend David Bryce.

1841   Works as a governess for the White family.

1842   Travels to Pensionnat Heger, Brussels, with Emily.

1843–48 Living at home with Emily and, later, Anne.

1845   Branwell dismissed from his post as tutor and begins serious decline into drink and drugs. Charlotte reads Emily's poems and suggests joint publication by Currer, Ellis, and Acton Bell.

1846   *Poems* by Currer, Ellis, and Acton Bell sells two copies. *Wuthering Heights* and *Agnes Grey* accepted for publication. *The Professor* frequently rejected. Begins writing *Jane Eyre* in Manchester.

1847   *Jane Eyre* finished and published by Smith, Elder & Co. Immediate success. Mixed reception for *Wuthering Heights*. Little notice taken of *Agnes Grey*.

1848   Charlotte and Anne visit London to dispel rumors that the three Bells are the same person. Branwell and Emily die of T.B.

1849   Anne dies of T.B. in Scarborough. *Shirley* published. Mixed reviews.

1851   Rejects proposal of James Taylor.

1852   *Villette* finished. Rejects proposal of Arthur Bell Nicholls, her father's curate.

1853	*Villette* published and favorably received.
1854	Marries Nicholls.
1855	Pregnant. Sickens and dies.
1857	Smith, Elder & Co. publish Elizabeth Gaskell's *Life of Charlotte Brontë*, which establishes the Brontë legend. They also finally publish *The Professor*.
1861	Patrick Brontë dies.
1906	Arthur Bell Nicholls dies.

FURTHER READING

CONTEMPORARY WORKS:

Brontë, Anne. *Agnes Grey*. New York: Penguin Classics, 1988.
Brontë, Anne. *The Tenant of Wildfell Hall*. New York: Penguin Classics, 1996.
Brontë, Charlotte. *Shirley*. New York: Penguin Classics, 1985.
Brontë, Charlotte. *Villette*. New York: Penguin Classics, 1985.
Brontë, Emily. *The Complete Poems*. New York: Penguin Classics, 1992.
Brontë, Emily. *Wuthering Heights*. New York: Penguin Classics, 1985.
Gaskell, Elizabeth. *The Life of Charlotte Brontë*. New York: Penguin Classics, 1975.

The poems of Currer, Ellis, and Acton Bell have recently been reprinted as *The Works of the Brontë Sisters*, with an introduction by Kathryn White, Ware, England: Wordsworth Poetry Library, 1995.

SECONDARY SOURCES:

Barker, Juliet. *The Brontës*. New York: St. Martin's Press, 1995.
Ford, Boris, ed. *From Dickens to Hardy*. Vol. 6 of *New Pelican Guide to English Literature*. New York: Penguin, 1993.
Gardiner, Juliet, ed. *The Brontës at Haworth: The World Within: A Life in Letters, Diaries and Writings*. New York: Crown, 1993.
Gordon, Lyndall. *Charlotte Brontë, A Passionate Life*. New York: W.W. Norton & Co., 1994.
Uglow, Jenny. *Elizabeth Gaskell: A Habit of Stories*. New York: Farrar, Straus & Giroux, 1993.
Winnifrith, T. *Charlotte & Emily Brontë*, vol. 1. New York: St. Martin's Press, 1994.
Winnifrith, T. *A New Life of Charlotte Brontë*. New York: St. Martin's Press, 1988.